Pumpkin Cocoon & Hat, *page 15*

Tab[illegible] Con[illegible]

GW01373062

Chunky Owl Cocoon & Hat, *page 5*

General Information

Mermaid Cocoon & Headband, *page 10*

Spiral Cocoon & Hat

Designs by Jessica Brown

Skill Level

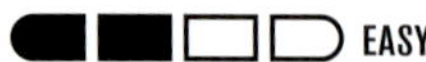 EASY

Finished Measurements

Cocoon: 13 inches long x 17 inches in circumference

Hat: 5 inches long x 11 inches in circumference at brim

Materials

- Premier Yarns Deborah Norville Everyday Soft Worsted medium (worsted) weight acrylic yarn (4 oz/203 yds/113g per ball):
  1 ball #1002 cream
- Size J/10/6mm crochet hook or size needed to obtain gauge
- Tapestry needle
- Stitch marker

4 MEDIUM

Gauge

Rnds 1–4 = 4½ inches

Pattern Notes

Refer to Stitch Diagrams as needed.

Weave in ends as work progresses.

Chain-2 at beginning of round counts as first half double crochet unless otherwise stated.

Work in continuous rounds; do not join or turn unless otherwise stated.

Mark first stitch of round. Move marker up with each round.

Join with slip stitch as indicated unless otherwise stated.

Cocoon

Rnd 1 (RS): Make a **slip ring** *(see illustration)*, **ch 2** *(see Pattern Notes)*, 9 hdc in ring. **Place marker** *(see Pattern Notes)*. Pull gently on beg tail to close sts. *(10 hdc)*

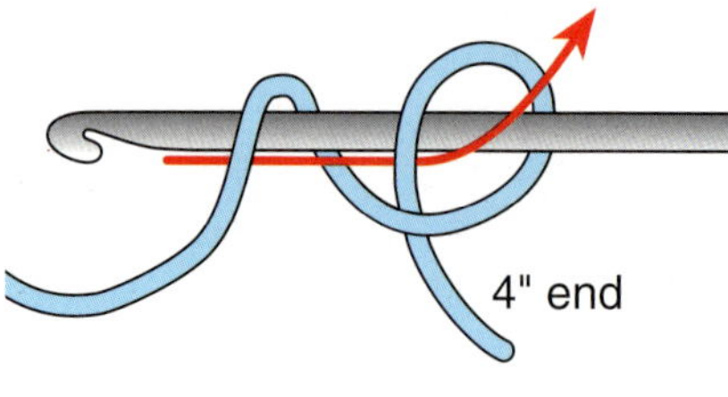

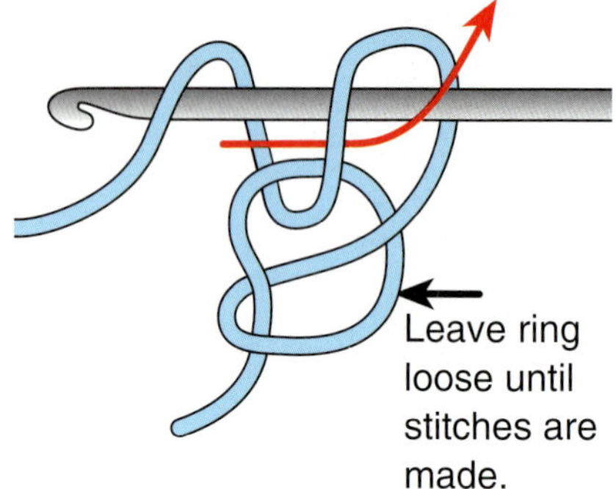

Slip Ring

Rnd 2: 2 hdc in each st around. *(20 hdc)*

Rnd 3: *2 hdc in next st, hdc in next st, rep from * around. *(30 hdc)*

Rnd 4: *2 hdc in next st, hdc in each of next 2 sts, rep from * around. *(40 hdc)*

Rnd 5: *2 hdc in next st, hdc in each of next 3 sts, rep from * around. *(50 hdc)*

Rnd 6: Hdc in each of next 4 sts, [ch 1, sk next st, hdc in each of next 4 sts] 9 times, ch 1, sk last st. *(40 hdc, 10 ch-1 sps)*

Rnds 7–25: Hdc in each of next 4 sts, [ch 1, sk next ch-1 sp, hdc in each of next 4 sts] 9 times, ch 1, sk last ch-1 sp.

Rnd 26: Hdc in each of next 4 sts, [ch 1, sk next ch-1 sp, hdc in each of next 4 sts] 9 times, ch 1, **join** *(see Pattern Notes)* in beg hdc.

Rnd 27: Sc in last ch-1 sp, sk next st, sc in each of next 3 sts, sc in next ch-1 sp, [sc in each of next 4 sts, sc in next ch-1 sp] 4 times, sk next st, sc in each of next 3 sts, [sc in next ch-1 sp, sc in each of next 4 sts] 4 times, join in beg sc. *(48 sc)*

Rnd 28: Ch 1, sc in each st around, join in beg sc. Fasten off.

Hat

Rnds 1 & 2: Rep rnds 1 and 2 of Cocoon.

Rnd 3: [Ch 1, sk next st, 2 hdc in next st] 10 times. *(20 hdc, 10 ch-1 sps)*

Rnd 4: [Ch 1, sk next ch-1 sp, 2 hdc in next st, hdc in next st] 10 times. *(30 hdc, 10 ch-1 sps)*

Rnds 5–9: [Ch 1, sk next ch-1 sp, hdc in each of next 3 sts] 10 times. At end of last rnd, **join** *(see Pattern Notes)* in next hdc.

Rnd 10: Ch 1, sc in each of first 3 sts, [sk next ch-1 sp, sc in each of next 3 sts] around, join in beg sc.

Rnd 11: Ch 1, sc in each st around, join in beg sc. Fasten off. ●

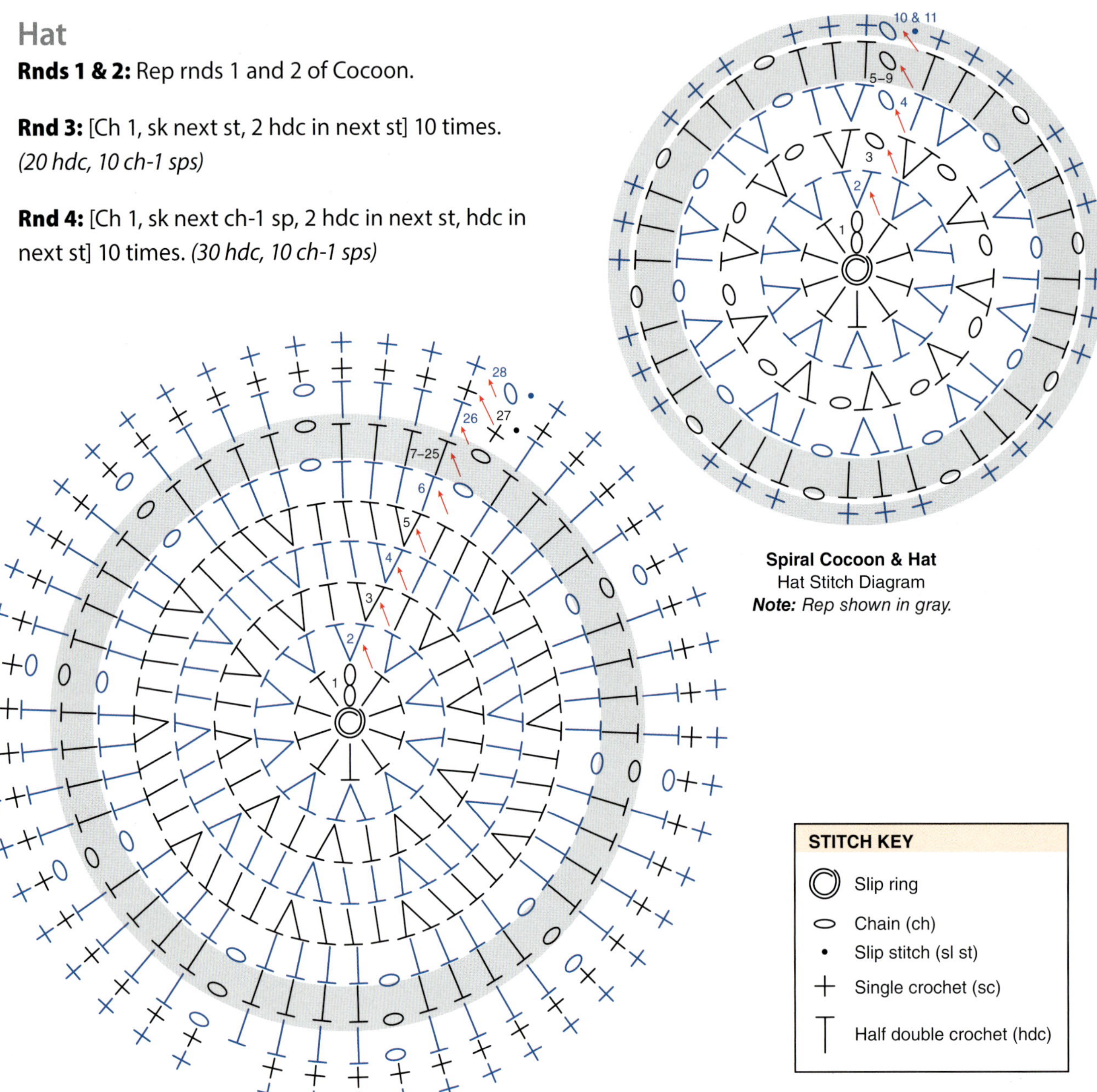

Spiral Cocoon & Hat
Hat Stitch Diagram
Note: *Rep shown in gray.*

Spiral Cocoon & Hat
Cocoon Stitch Diagram
Note: *Rep shown in gray.*

Chunky Owl Cocoon & Hat

Designs by Ira Rott

Skill Level

EASY

Finished Measurements

Cocoon: 13 inches long x 20 inches in circumference

Hat: 5 inches long x 14 inches in circumference

Materials

- Red Heart Snuggle Bunny super bulky (super chunky) weight acrylic yarn (4 oz/83 yds/113g per ball):
  1 ball #9802 bluebird

- Red Heart Super Saver medium (worsted) weight acrylic yarn (7 oz/364 yds/198g per skein):
  1 skein each #320 cornmeal, #365 coffee, #373 petal pink, #672 spring green and #718 shocking pink

- Sizes E/4/3.5mm, I/9/5.5mm and K/10½/6.5mm crochet hooks or size needed to obtain gauge
- Tapestry needle
- Polyester fiberfill
- 4-inch piece of cardboard

Gauge

Size K hook: 9 dc sts = 4 inches; 5 rows = 4 inches

Pattern Notes

Refer to Stitch Diagrams as needed.

Weave in ends as work progresses.

Join with slip stitch as indicated unless otherwise stated.

Chain-2 at beginning of round does not count as a stitch unless otherwise stated.

Chain-3 at beginning of round does not count as a stitch unless otherwise stated.

Special Stitches

Single crochet join (sc join): Place a slip knot on hook, insert hook in indicated st, yo and draw up a lp, yo and pull through both lps on hook.

Back slip stitch (back sl st): On WS, insert hook under both vertical bars of indicated st, yo and pull through 3 lps on hook.

Shell: Ch 3, 2 dc in indicated st.

Cocoon

Rnd 1 (RS): With size K hook and bluebird, form a **slip ring** *(see illustration)*, ch 1, 11 sc in ring, **join** *(see Pattern Notes)* in beg sc. Pull gently on beg tail to close sts. *(11 sc)*

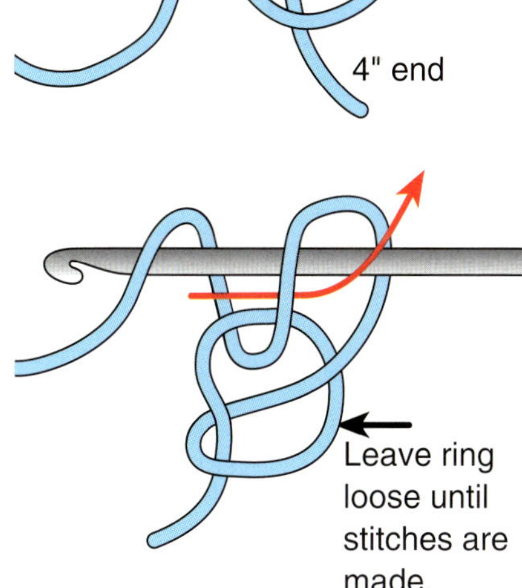

Slip Ring

Rnd 2: Ch 2 *(see Pattern Notes)*, 2 dc in each st around, join in beg dc. *(22 dc)*

Rnd 3: Ch 2, dc in first st, 2 dc in next st, [dc in next st, 2 dc in next st] 10 times, join in beg dc. *(33 dc)*

Rnd 4: Ch 2, dc in each of first 2 sts, 2 dc in next st, [dc in each of next 2 sts, 2 dc in next st] 10 times, join in beg dc. *(44 dc)*

Rnds 5–15: Ch 2, dc in each st around, join in beg dc. Fasten off.

Rnd 16: Sc join *(see Special Stitches)* cornmeal in any st, ch 1, sc in each st around, join in beg sc. Fasten off.

Rnd 17: Sc join shocking pink in any st, sc in each st around, join in beg sc. Fasten off.

Rnd 18: Sc join green in any st, sc in each st around, join in beg sc. Fasten off.

Rnd 19: Sc join petal pink in any st, **reverse sc** *(see Stitch Guide)* in each st around, join in beg sc. Fasten off.

Flower

Rnd 1 (RS): With size I hook and cornmeal, form a slip ring, ch 1, 6 sc in ring. Pull gently on beg tail to close sts. *(6 sc)*

Rnd 2: 2 sc in each st around. *(12 sc)*

Rnds 3 & 4: Sc in each st around. At end of rnd 4, join in beg sc. Leaving a long tail for sewing, fasten off.

Rnd 5: Join petal pink in any st, [**ch 3**—*see Pattern Notes),* 3 dc in next st, ch 3, sl st in next st—*petal made)*] 6 times. Fasten off. *(6 petals)*

Rnd 6: With green, **back sl st** *(see Special Stitches)* in any sl st, ch 5, sk next 3 dc, [back sl st in next sl st, ch 5, sk next 3 dc] 5 times, join in beg sl st. *(6 ch-5 sps)*

Rnd 7: Holding ch-5 sps behind petals, [ch 3, 6 dc in next ch-5 sp, ch 3, sl st in next sl st—*petal made)*] 6 times, ending last rep in beg sl st. Fasten off. *(6 petals)*

Rnd 8: With shocking pink, back sl st in any sl st, ch 7, sk next 6 dc, [back sl st in next sl st, ch 7, sk next 6 dc] 5 times, join in beg sl st. *(6 ch-7 sps)*

Rnd 9: Holding ch-7 sps behind petals, [ch 3, 9 dc in next ch-7 sp, ch 3, sl st in next sl st (*petal made)*] 6 times, ending last rep in beg sl st. Leaving a long tail for sewing, fasten off. *(6 petals)*

Position Flower near top edge of Cocoon. With cornmeal tail and sewing through all thicknesses, **backstitch** *(see illustration)* around rnd 4 of Flower. Stuff with fiberfill before completing backstitching.

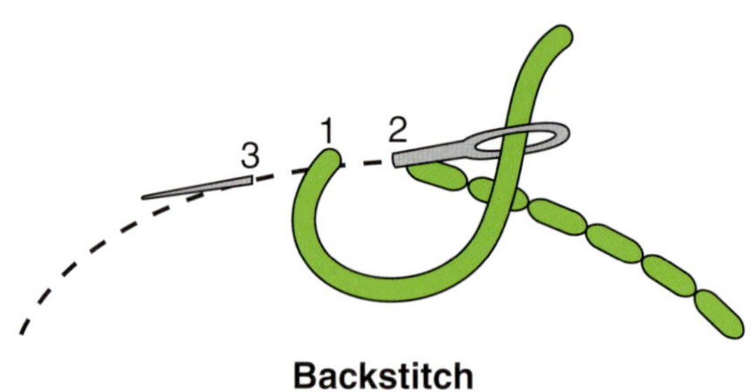

Backstitch

With shocking pink tail and working in rnd 9, ***whipstitch** *(see illustration)* in sl st between next 2 Petals, insert needle through base of each of next 9 dc and pull yarn through to next sl st, rep from * around. Secure tail in first st.

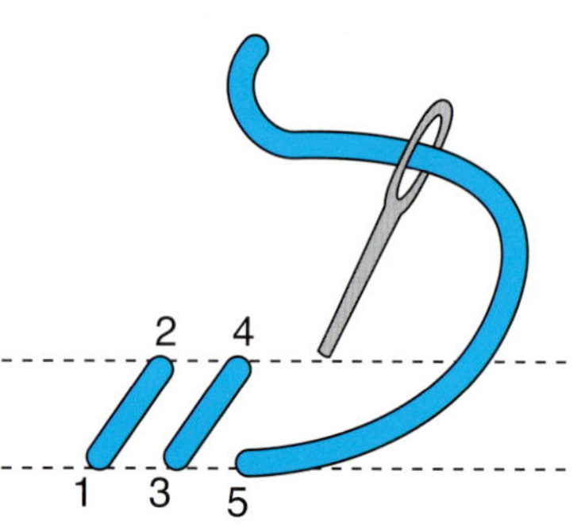

Whipstitch

Hat

Rnd 1 (RS): With size K hook and bluebird, form a slip ring, ch 1, 10 sc in ring, **join** *(see Pattern Notes)* in beg sc. *(10 sc)*

Rnd 2: Ch 2 *(see Pattern Notes)*, 2 dc in each st around, join in beg dc. *(20 dc)*

Rnd 3: Ch 2, dc in first st, 2 dc in next st, [dc in next st, 2 dc in next st] 9 times, join in beg dc. *(30 dc)*

Rnd 4: Ch 2, dc in each of first 14 sts, 2 dc in next st, dc in each of next 14 sts, 2 dc in next st, join in beg dc. *(32 dc)*

Rnds 5 & 6: Ch 2, dc in each st around, join in beg dc. At end of rnd 6, fasten off.

Mermaid Cocoon & Headband

Designs by Bonnie Potter

Skill Level

Finished Measurements

Cocoon: 13 inches long, excluding tail, x 16 inches in circumference

Headband: 1½ inches wide x 12 inches in circumference

Materials

- Premier Yarns Deborah Norville Everyday Soft Worsted medium (worsted) weight acrylic yarn (4 oz/203 yds/113g per ball):
  1 ball each #1002 cream, #1015 sagebrush and #1026 grenadine
- Size J/10/6mm crochet hook or size needed to obtain gauge
- Tapestry needle

Gauge

12 hdc = 4 inches; 10 rows = 4 inches

Pattern Notes

Refer to Stitch Diagrams as needed.

Weave in ends as work progresses.

Chain-2 at beginning of row or round counts as first half double crochet unless otherwise stated.

Join with slip stitch as indicated unless otherwise stated.

To custom-fit Headband, chain multiples of 6 until chain fits snugly around Baby's head. Designer recommends 36 chains for newborn and 42 chains for 3–6-week-old baby.

Chain-3 at beginning of round does not count as a stitch unless otherwise stated.

Special Stitches

Shell: 5 dc in indicated st.

Reverse slip stitch (reverse sl st): With yarn in front of hook, insert hook from back to front where indicated, yo, draw through all sts and lp on hook.

Picot: Ch 3, sl st in 3rd ch from hook.

Cocoon

Tail

Row 1: With sagebrush, ch 3, 2 hdc in 3rd ch from hook *(beg 2 sk chs count as first hdc)*, turn. *(3 hdc)*

Row 2: Ch 2 *(see Pattern Notes)*, hdc in same st as beg ch-2, hdc in next st, 2 hdc in top of beg ch-2, turn. *(5 hdc)*

Row 3: Ch 2, hdc in same st as beg ch-2, hdc in each of next 3 sts, 2 hdc in top of beg ch-2, turn. *(7 hdc)*

Row 4: Ch 2, hdc in same st as beg ch-2, hdc in each of next 5 sts, 2 hdc in top of beg ch-2, turn. *(9 hdc)*

Rows 5–9: Ch 2, hdc in each st across, turn.

Row 10: Ch 1, sk first st, hdc in each of next 6 sts, **hdc dec** *(see Stitch Guide)* in next st and top of beg ch-2, turn. *(7 sts)*

Row 11: Ch 1, sk first st, hdc in each of next 4 sts, hdc dec in next 2 sts, turn. *(5 sts)*

Row 12: Ch 2, hdc in each st across, turn.

Rows 13–21: Rep rows 3–11.

Row 22: Ch 1, hdc in each of next 2 sts, hdc dec in last 2 sts, turn. *(3 hdc)*

Row 23: Ch 1, hdc dec in last 2 sts. **Do not fasten off**. *(1 hdc)*

Rnd 24: Now working in rnd, ch 1, work 33 sc evenly sp across ends of rows, (sc, ch 3, sc) in opposite side of ch of row 1, working in ends of rows of 2nd side, work 15 sc evenly sp to row 12, 3 dc in row 12, work 15 sc evenly sp across, (sc, ch 3, sc) in hdc of row 23, **join** *(see Pattern Notes)* in beg sc. Fasten off. *(65 sc, 3 dc, 2 ch-3 sps)*

Body

Rnd 1: With RS of dc facing and working in **front lps** *(see Stitch Guide)*, join sagebrush in first dc, ch 2, hdc in each of next 2 dc, turn, hdc in each unworked lp, join in top of beg ch-2. *(6 hdc)*

Rnd 2: Ch 2, hdc in same st as beg ch-2, hdc in next st, [2 hdc in next st, hdc in next st] twice, join in top of beg ch-2. *(9 hdc)*

Rnd 3: Ch 2, hdc in same st as beg ch-2, hdc in each of next 2 sts, [2 hdc in next st, hdc in each of next 2 sts] twice, join in top of beg ch-2. *(12 hdc)*

Rnd 4: Ch 2, hdc in same st as beg ch-2, hdc in next st, [2 hdc in next st, hdc in next st] 5 times, join in top of beg ch-2. *(18 hdc)*

Rnd 5: Ch 2, hdc in same st as beg ch-2, hdc in each of next 2 sts, [2 hdc in next st, hdc in each of next 2 sts] 5 times, join in top of beg ch-2. *(24 hdc)*

Rnd 6: Ch 2, hdc in each st around, join in top of beg ch-2.

Rnd 7: Ch 2, hdc in same st as beg ch-2, hdc in each of next 3 sts, [2 hdc in next st, hdc in each of next 3 sts] 5 times, join in top of beg ch-2. *(30 hdc)*

Rnd 8: Ch 2, hdc in same st as beg ch-2, hdc in each of next 4 sts, [2 hdc in next st, hdc in each of next 4 sts] 5 times, join in top of beg ch-2. *(36 hdc)*

Rnd 9: Rep rnd 6.

Rnd 10: Ch 2, hdc in same st as beg ch-2, hdc in each of next 5 sts, [2 hdc in next st, hdc in each of next 5 sts] 5 times, join in top of beg ch-2. *(42 hdc)*

Rnd 11: Rep rnd 6.

Rnd 12: Ch 2, hdc in same st as beg ch-2, hdc in each of next 6 sts, [2 hdc in next st, hdc in each of next 6 sts] 5 times, join in top of beg ch-2. *(48 hdc)*

Rnds 13–35: Rep rnd 6.

Rnd 36: Ch 1, sc in same ch as beg ch-1, *sk next 2 sts, **shell** *(see Special Stitches)* in next st, sk next 2 sts**, sc in next st, rep from * around, ending last rep at **, join in beg sc. Fasten off. *(8 sc, 8 shells)*

Headband

Rnd 1: With cream, **ch 36** *(see Pattern Notes)*, taking care not to twist sts, **join** *(see Pattern Notes)* in first ch to form a ring, ch 1, sc in first ch, *sk next 2 chs, shell in next ch, sk next 2 chs**, sc in next ch, rep from * around, ending last rep at **, join in beg sc. *(6 sc, 6 shells)*

Rnd 2: Ch 3 *(see Pattern Notes)*, working on opposite side of foundation ch, sc in first ch, *sk next 2 chs, shell in next ch, sk next 2 chs**, sc in next ch, rep from * around, ending last rep at **, join in beg sc. Fasten off. *(6 sc, 6 shells)*

Flower

Rnd 1 (RS): With grenadine, ch 4, join in first ch to form a ring, ch 1, (sc, hdc, 4 dc, hdc, sc) in ring *(center petal made)*.

Note: *On following rnd, work reverse sl sts in beg ring in sps between sts of rnd 1.*

Rnd 2: Ch 2, working behind petal sts, **reverse sl st** *(see Special Stitches)* between first sc and next hdc, [ch 2, sk next sp, reverse sl st in beg ring] 3 times, ch 2, join in beg ch-2 sp. *(5 ch-2 sps)*

Rnd 3: Ch 2, (2 dc, ch 2, sl st) in first ch-2 sp, (sl st, ch 2, 2 dc, ch 2, sl st) in each rem ch-2 sp, join in beg sl st. *(5 petals)*

Note: *On following rnd, working between sts of rnd 3, work reverse sl sts in corresponding ch-2 sps on rnd 2.*

Rnd 4: Ch 1, working behind petals, reverse sl st between beg ch-2 of first petal and next dc, ch 3, reverse sl st between next dc and last ch-2 of same petal, [ch 3, reverse sl st between beg ch-2 and first dc of next petal, ch 3, reverse sl st between next dc and last ch-2 of same petal] 4 times, ch 3, join in beg ch-3 sp. *(10 ch-3 sps)*

Rnd 5: Ch 2, (3 dc, ch 2, sl st) in same ch-3 sp as beg ch-2, (sl st, ch 2, 3 dc, ch 2, sl st) in each rem ch-3 sp around, join in base of beg ch-2. Fasten off. *(10 petals)*

Leaf

Make 2.

With sagebrush, ch 6, sc in 2nd ch from hook, hdc in next ch, dc in each of next 2 chs, (4 dc, **picot**—*see Special Stitches*, 4 dc) in next ch, working on opposite side of foundation ch, sk first ch, dc in each of next 2 chs, hdc in next ch, sc in last ch, join in first sc. Fasten off. ●

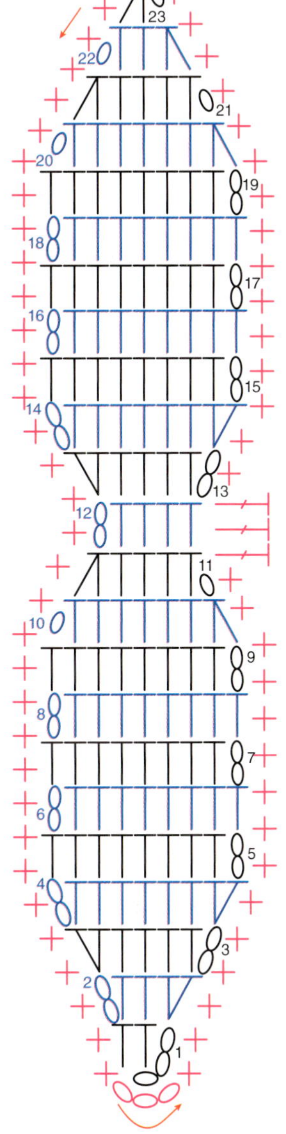

Mermaid Cocoon & Headband
Cocoon Tail Stitch Diagram

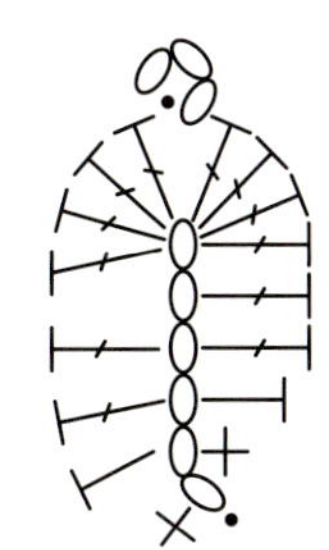

Mermaid Cocoon & Headband
Leaf Stitch Diagram

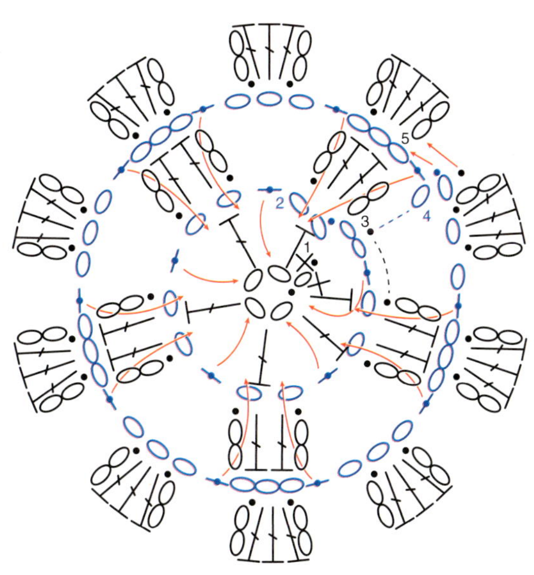

Mermaid Cocoon & Headband
Flower Stitch Diagram

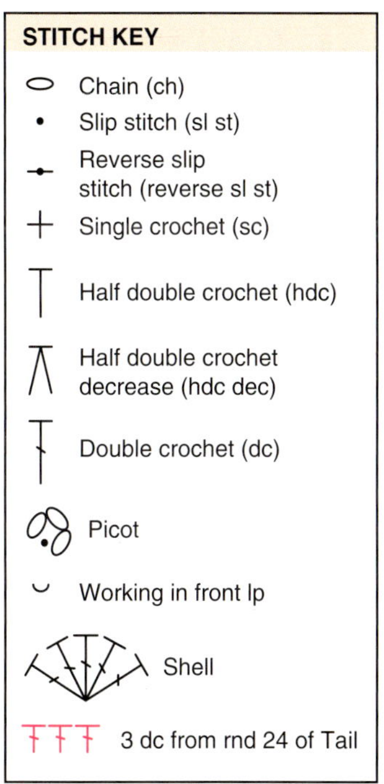

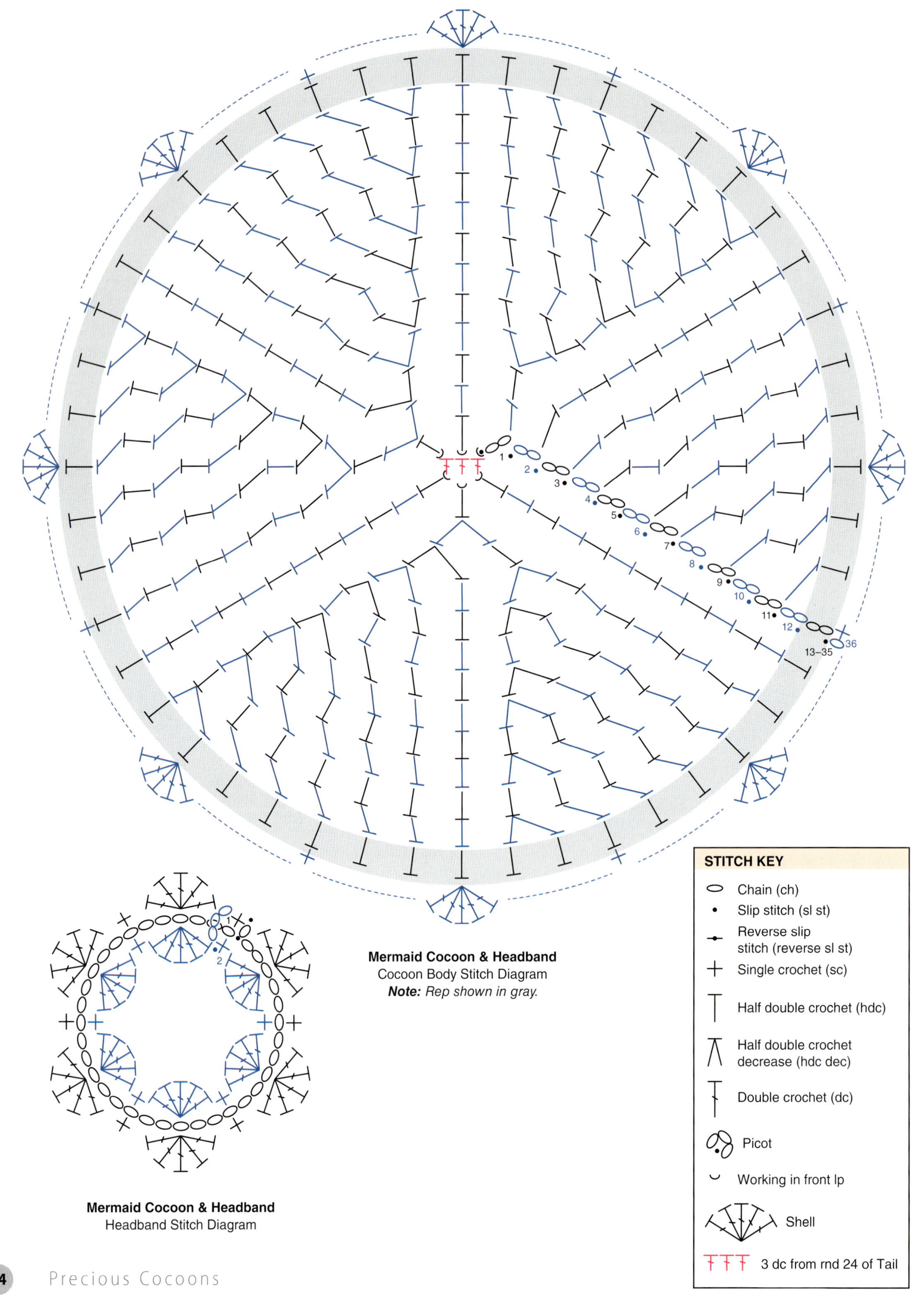

Mermaid Cocoon & Headband
Cocoon Body Stitch Diagram
Note: *Rep shown in gray.*

Mermaid Cocoon & Headband
Headband Stitch Diagram

Pumpkin Cocoon & Hat

Designs by Rachel Choi

Skill Level

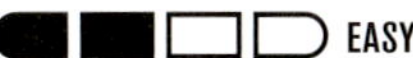

Finished Measurements

Cocoon: 20 inches long x 20 inches in circumference

Hat: 5 inches long, excluding stem, x 14 inches in circumference

Materials

- Premier Yarns Deborah Norville Everyday Soft Worsted medium (worsted) weight acrylic yarn (4 oz/203 yds/113g per ball):
  - 3 balls #1022 bittersweet
  - 1 ball #1029 shamrock
- Size I/9/5.5mm crochet hook or size needed to obtain gauge
- Tapestry needle
- Stitch marker

Gauge

14 dc = 4 inches; 10 rows = 4 inches

Pattern Notes

Refer to Stitch Diagrams as needed.

Weave in ends as work progresses.

Work in continuous rounds; do not join or turn unless otherwise stated.

Mark first stitch of round. Move marker up with each round.

Join with slip stitch as indicated unless otherwise stated.

Cocoon

Rnd 1 (RS): With bittersweet, ch 3, 12 dc in 3rd ch from hook *(beg sk chs do not count as a st).* **Place marker** *(see Pattern Notes). (12 dc)*

Rnd 2: 2 dc in each dc around. *(24 dc)*

Rnd 3: [**Fpdc**—*see Stitch Guide*) around next dc, 2 dc in next dc] around. *(12 fpdc, 24 dc)*

Rnd 4: [Fpdc around next fpdc, 2 dc in next dc, dc in next dc] around. *(12 fpdc, 36 dc)*

Rnd 5: [Fpdc around next fpdc, 2 dc in next dc, dc in each of next 2 dc] around. *(12 fpdc, 48 dc)*

Rnd 6: [Fpdc around next fpdc, 2 dc in next dc, dc in each of next 3 dc] around. *(12 fpdc, 60 dc)*

Rnds 7–52: [Fpdc around next fpdc, dc in each of next 5 dc] around.

Rnd 53: Sc in each st around, **join** *(see Pattern Notes)* in beg sc. Fasten off. *(72 sc)*

Hat

Rnds 1–4: Rep rnds 1–4 of Cocoon.

Rnds 5–12: [Fpdc around next fpdc, dc in each of next 3 dc] around.

Rnd 13: Rep rnd 53 of Cocoon. *(48 sc)*

Stem

Rnd 1 (RS): With shamrock, ch 3, 6 dc in 3rd ch from hook. Place marker. *(6 dc)*

Rnds 2 & 3: Dc in each dc around.

Rnd 4: Sc in each dc around.

Rnd 5: [Ch 5, sl st in 5th ch from hook, sc in next sc] 6 times. Leaving a long tail for sewing, fasten off. *(6 sc)*

Sew Stem to top of Hat. ●

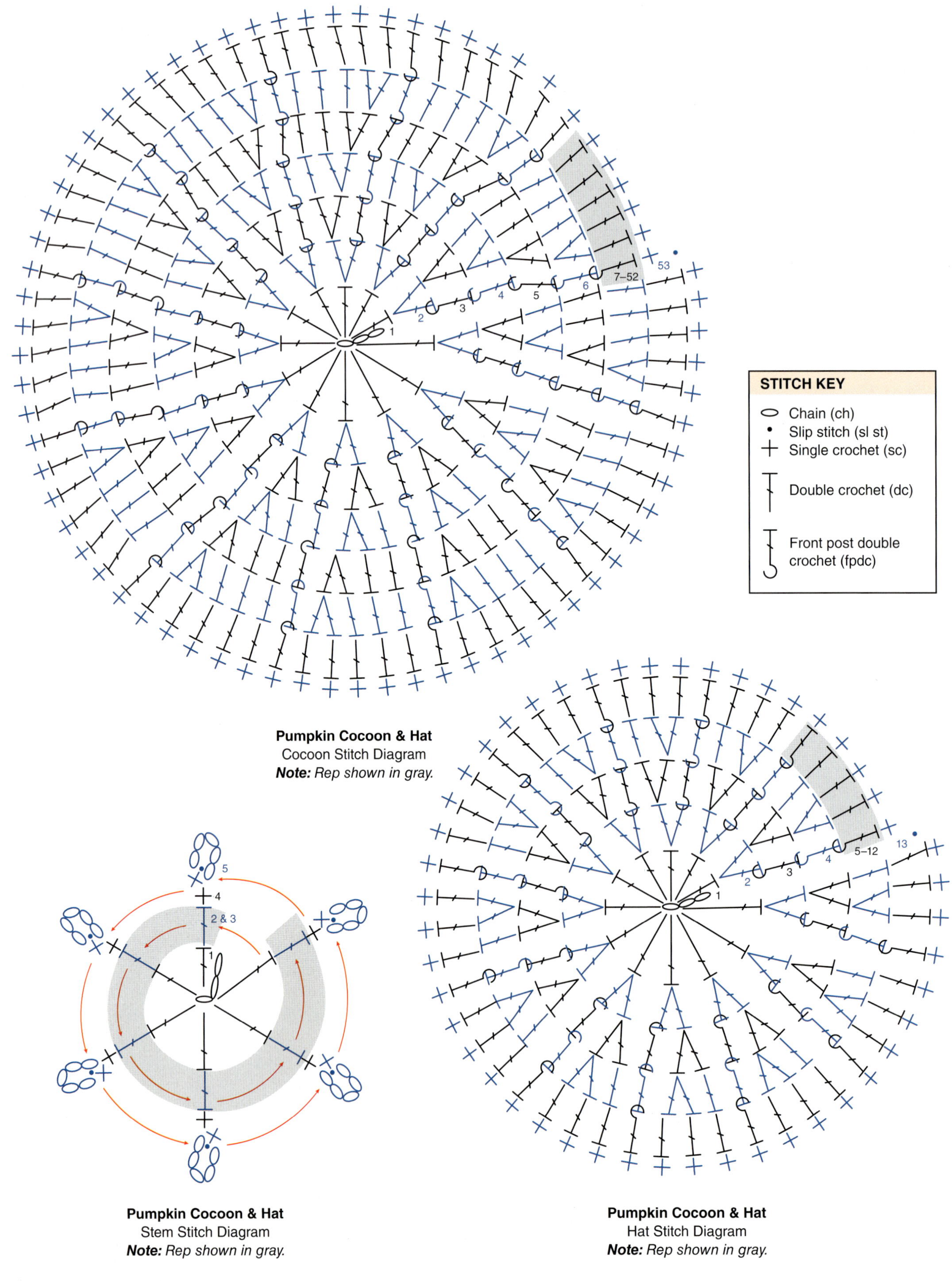

Pumpkin Cocoon & Hat
Cocoon Stitch Diagram
Note: *Rep shown in gray.*

Pumpkin Cocoon & Hat
Stem Stitch Diagram
Note: *Rep shown in gray.*

Pumpkin Cocoon & Hat
Hat Stitch Diagram
Note: *Rep shown in gray.*

Santa Stocking Cocoon & Hat

Designs by Christine Naugle

Skill Level

 EASY

Finished Measurements

Cocoon: 13½ inches long x 13 inches in circumference

Hat: 10½ inches long, excluding Pompom, x 11 inches in circumference at brim

Materials

- Premier Yarns Deborah Norville Everyday Soft Worsted medium (worsted) weight acrylic yarn (4 oz/203 yds/113g per ball):
  - 1 ball each #1001 snow white and #1007 really red
- Size K/10½/6.5mm crochet hook or size needed to obtain gauge
- Tapestry needle
- 2½-inch pompom maker

Gauge

12 hdc = 4 inches; 7 rows = 3 inches

Pattern Notes

Refer to Stitch Diagrams as needed.

Weave in ends as work progresses.

Chain-2 at beginning of round counts as first half double crochet unless otherwise stated.

Join with slip stitch as indicated unless otherwise stated.

Work front post stitches loosely.

Cocoon

Row 1: With red, ch 25, sc in 2nd ch from hook and in each ch across, turn. *(24 sc)*

Rnd 2 (RS): Now working in rnds, **ch 2** *(see Pattern Notes)*, hdc in each st across, 2 hdc in end of row, working in opposite side of foundation ch, hdc in each ch across to last st, 2 hdc in last st, **join** *(see Pattern Notes)* in top of beg ch-2. *(52 hdc)*

Rnd 3: Ch 2, hdc in each of next 22 sts, 2 hdc in each of next 6 sts, hdc in each of last 23 sts, join in top of beg ch-2. *(58 hdc)*

Rnds 4 & 5: Ch 2, hdc in same st as beg ch-2, hdc in each rem st around, join in top of beg ch-2. *(60 hdc)*

Rnd 6: Ch 2, hdc in each of next 25 sts, dc in each of next 10 sts, hdc in each of next 24 sts, join in top of beg ch-2. *(50 hdc, 10 dc)*

Rnd 7: Ch 2, hdc in each of next 25 sts, [**dc dec** *(see Stitch Guide)* in next 2 sts] 5 times, hdc in each of last 24 sts, join in top of beg ch-2. *(50 hdc, 5 dc dec)*

Rnd 8: Ch 2, hdc in each of next 24 sts, dc dec in next 2 sts, dc dec in next 3 sts, dc dec in next 2 sts, hdc in each of last 23 sts, join in top of beg ch-2. *(48 hdc, 3 dc dec)*

Rnd 9: Ch 2, hdc in each of next 22 sts, [dc dec in next 2 sts] 4 times, hdc in each of last 21 sts, join in top of beg ch-2. *(44 hdc, 4 dc)*

Rnd 10: Ch 2, hdc in each of next 20 sts, [dc dec in next 2 sts] 4 times, hdc in each of last 19 sts, join in top of beg ch-2. *(40 hdc, 4 dc dec)*

Rnd 11: Ch 2, hdc in each of next 18 sts, dc dec in next 2 sts, dc dec in next 3 sts, dc dec in next 2 sts, hdc in each of last 18 sts, join in top of beg ch-2. *(37 hdc, 3 dc dec)*

Rnds 12–28: Ch 2, hdc in each st around, **changing color** *(see Stitch Guide)* to white in last hdc of last rnd, join in top of beg ch-2. *(40 hdc)*

Rnds 29–33: Ch 2, **fphdc** *(see Stitch Guide and Pattern Notes)* around each st around, join in top of beg ch-2. At end of last rnd, fasten off.

Hat

Rnd 1 (RS): With red, ch 3, 4 hdc in 3rd ch from hook *(beg 2 sk chs count as a hdc)*, **join** *(see Pattern Notes)* in 2nd beg sk ch. *(5 hdc)*

Rnds 2–16: Ch 2 *(see Pattern Notes)*, hdc in same st as beg ch-2, hdc in each rem st around, join in top of beg ch-2. *(20 hdc)*

Rnd 17: Ch 2, hdc in same st as beg ch-2, hdc in each of next 4 sts, [2 hdc in next st, hdc in each of next 4 sts] 3 times, join in top of beg ch-2. *(24 hdc)*

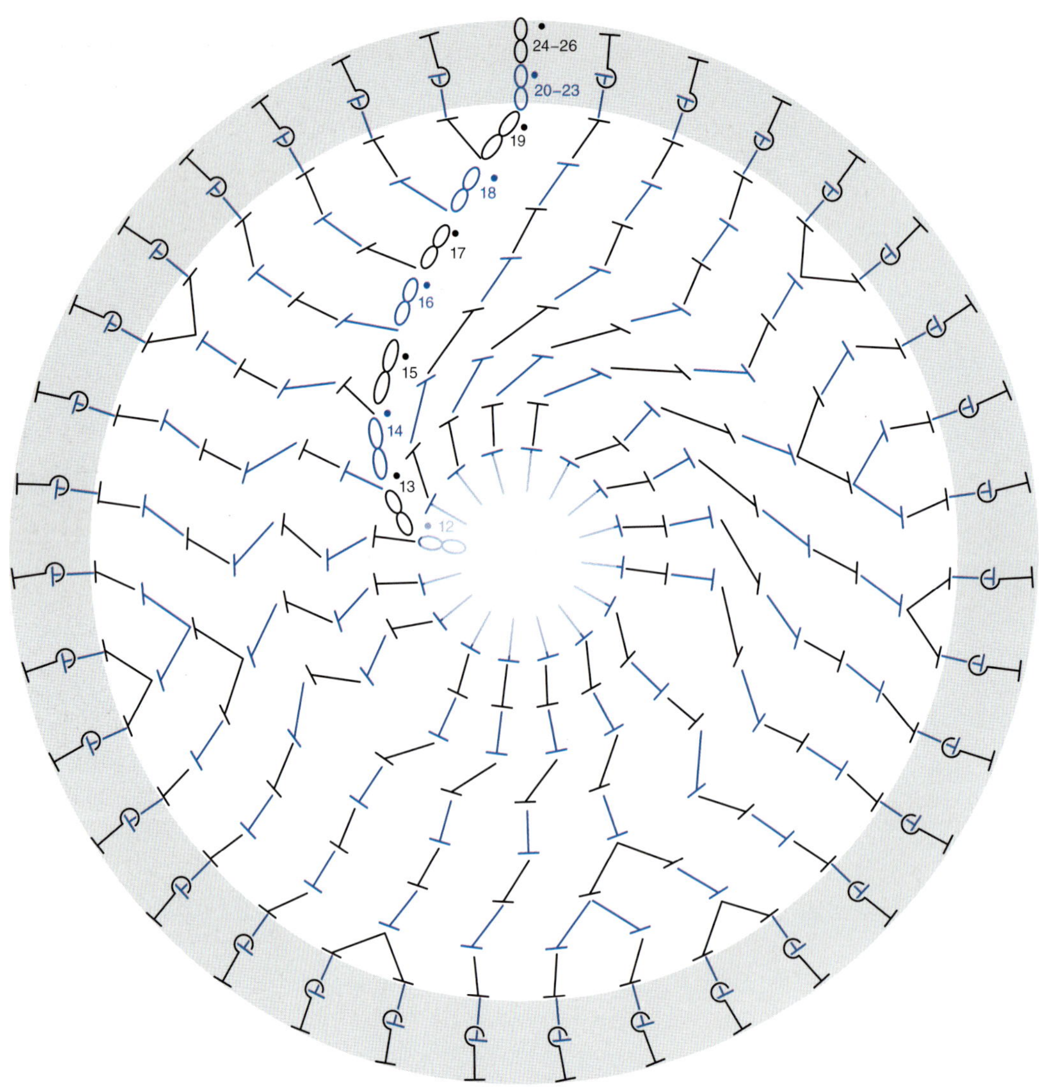

Santa Stocking Cocoon & Hat
Body & Brim of Hat Stitch Diagram
Note: *Rep shown in gray.*

Rnd 18: Ch 2, hdc in same st as beg ch-2, hdc in each of next 5 sts, [2 hdc in next st, hdc in each of next 5 sts] 3 times, join in top of beg ch-2. *(28 hdc)*

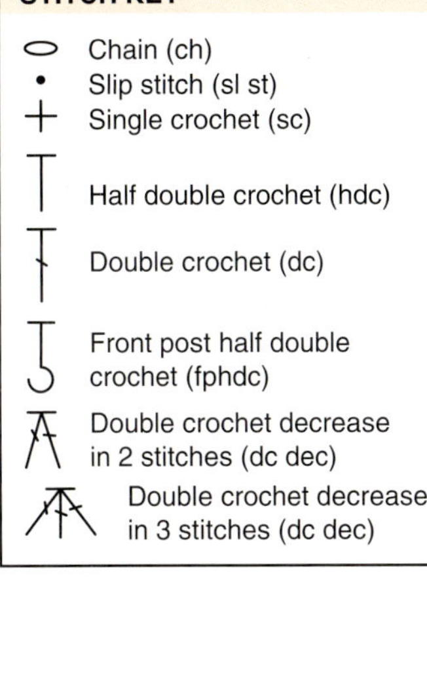

Rnd 19: Ch 2, hdc in same st as beg ch-2, hdc in each of next 3 sts, [2 hdc in next st, hdc in each of next 3 sts] 6 times, join in top of beg ch-2. *(35 hdc)*

Rnds 20–23: Ch 2, hdc in each st around, changing color to white in last hdc of last rnd, join in top of beg ch-2.

Rnds 24–26: Ch 2, **fphdc** *(see Stitch Guide and Pattern Notes)* around each st around, join in top of beg ch-2. At end of last rnd, fasten off.

Pompom

Following manufacturer's directions, with white, make a 2½-inch Pompom. Tie Pompom to rnd 1 of Hat. ●

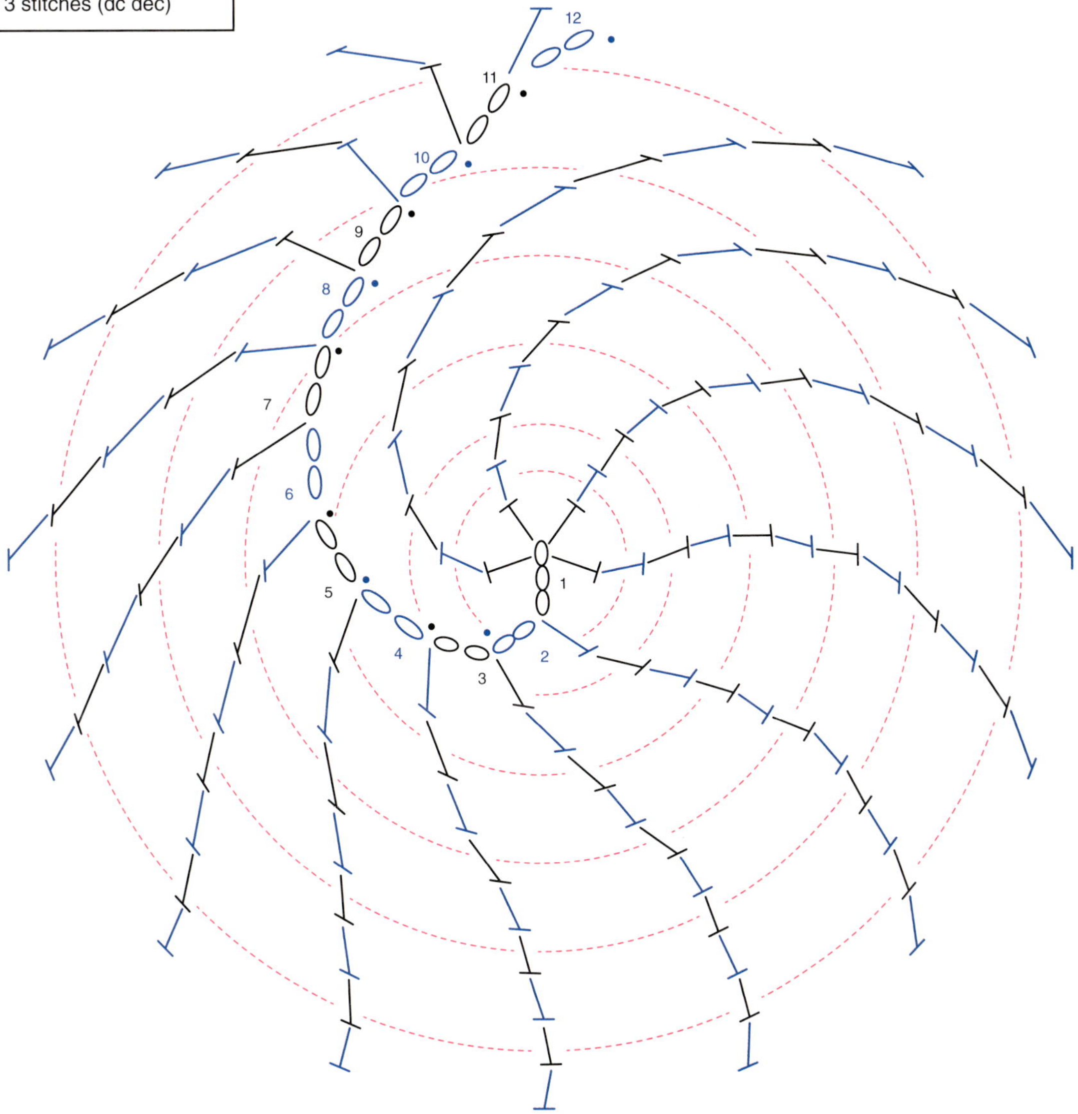

Santa Stocking Cocoon & Hat
Tip of Hat Stitch Diagram

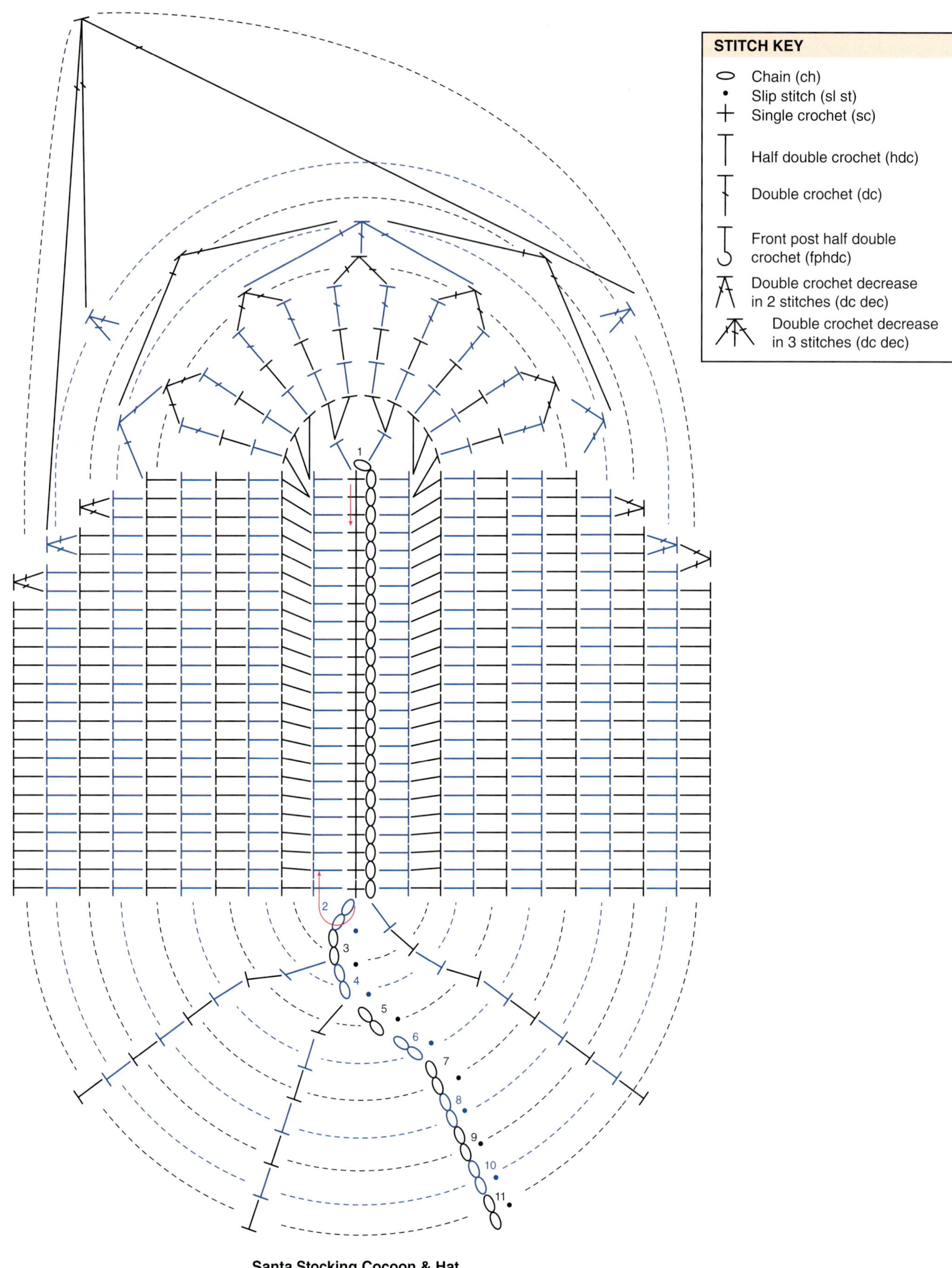

Santa Stocking Cocoon & Hat
Base of Cocoon Stitch Diagram

STITCH GUIDE

Need help? ▶ **StitchGuide.com** • ILLUSTRATED GUIDES • HOW-TO VIDEOS

STITCH ABBREVIATIONS

beg .... begin/begins/beginning
bpdc .... back post double crochet
bpsc .... back post single crochet
bptr .... back post treble crochet
CC .... contrasting color
ch(s) .... chain(s)
ch- .... refers to chain or space previously made (i.e., ch-1 space)
ch sp(s) .... chain space(s)
cl(s) .... cluster(s)
cm .... centimeter(s)
dc .... double crochet (singular/plural)
dc dec .... double crochet 2 or more stitches together, as indicated
dec .... decrease/decreases/decreasing
dtr .... double treble crochet
ext .... extended
fpdc .... front post double crochet
fpsc .... front post single crochet
fptr .... front post treble crochet
g .... gram(s)
hdc .... half double crochet
hdc dec .... half double crochet 2 or more stitches together, as indicated
inc .... increase/increases/increasing
lp(s) .... loop(s)
MC .... main color
mm .... millimeter(s)
oz .... ounce(s)
pc .... popcorn(s)
rem .... remain/remains/remaining
rep(s) .... repeat(s)
rnd(s) .... round(s)
RS .... right side
sc .... single crochet (singular/plural)
sc dec .... single crochet 2 or more stitches together, as indicated
sk .... skip/skipped/skipping
sl st(s) .... slip stitch(es)
sp(s) .... space(s)/spaced
st(s) .... stitch(es)
tog .... together
tr .... treble crochet
trtr .... triple treble
WS .... wrong side
yd(s) .... yard(s)
yo .... yarn over

YARN CONVERSION

OUNCES TO GRAMS		GRAMS TO OUNCES	
1	28.4	25	⅞
2	56.7	40	1⅔
3	85.0	50	1¾
4	113.4	100	3½

UNITED STATES		UNITED KINGDOM
sl st (slip stitch)	=	sc (single crochet)
sc (single crochet)	=	dc (double crochet)
hdc (half double crochet)	=	htr (half treble crochet)
dc (double crochet)	=	tr (treble crochet)
tr (treble crochet)	=	dtr (double treble crochet)
dtr (double treble crochet)	=	ttr (triple treble crochet)
skip	=	miss

Reverse single crochet (reverse sc): Ch 1, sk first st, working from left to right, insert hook in next st from front to back, draw up lp on hook, yo and draw through both lps on hook.

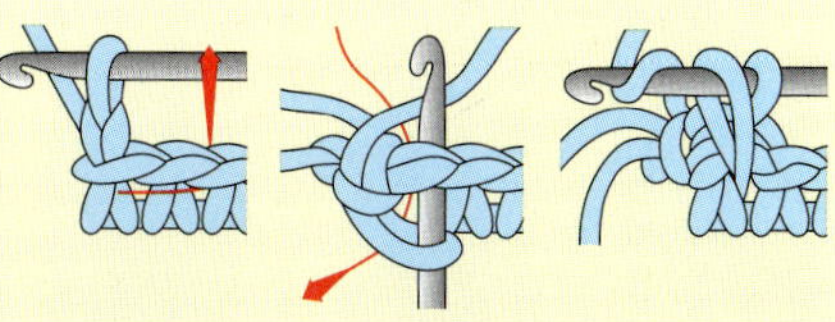

Chain (ch): Yo, pull through lp on hook.

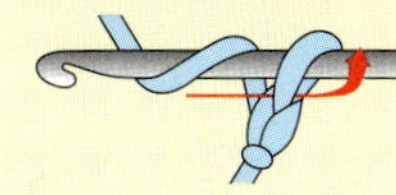

Single crochet (sc): Insert hook in st, yo, pull through st, yo, pull through both lps on hook.

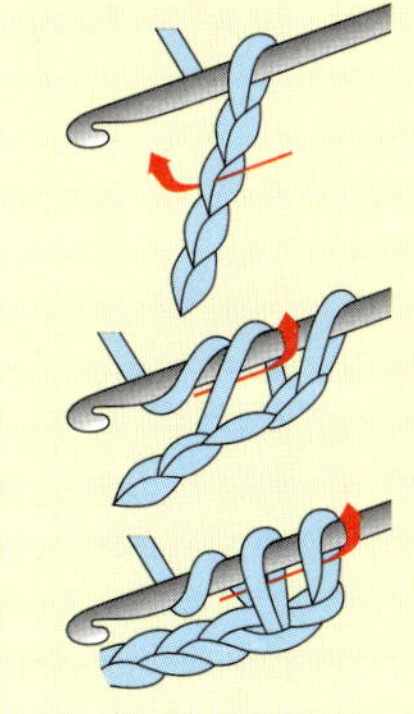

Double crochet (dc): Yo, insert hook in st, yo, pull through st, [yo, pull through 2 lps] twice.

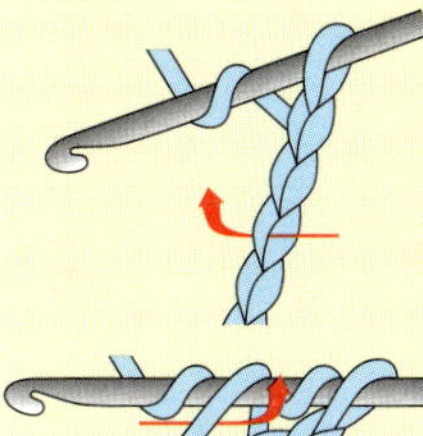

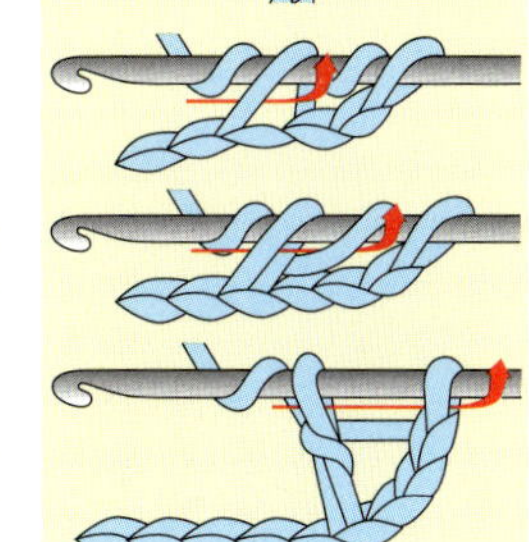

Front loop (front lp) Back loop (back lp)

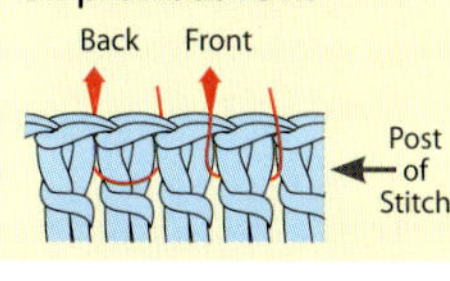

Front post stitch (fp): Back post stitch (bp): When working post st, insert hook from right to left around post of st on previous row.

Half double crochet (hdc): Yo, insert hook in st, yo, pull through st, yo, pull through all 3 lps on hook.

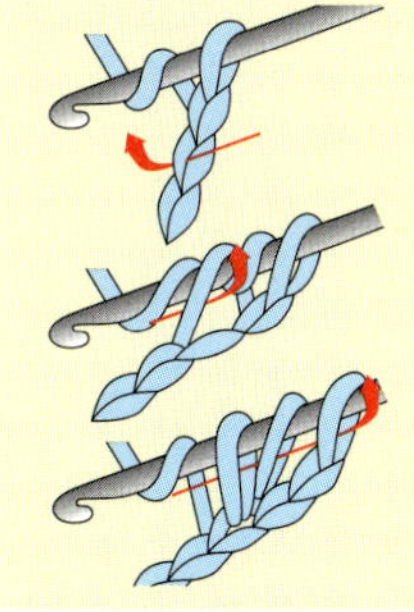

Double treble crochet (dtr): Yo 3 times, insert hook in st, yo, pull through st, [yo, pull through 2 lps] 4 times.

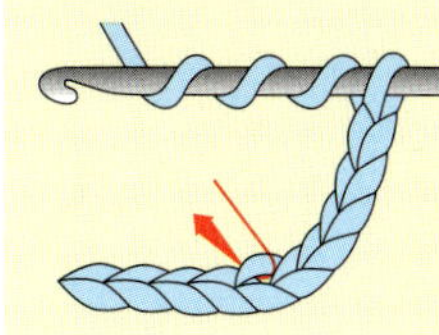

Slip stitch (sl st): Insert hook in st, pull through both lps on hook.

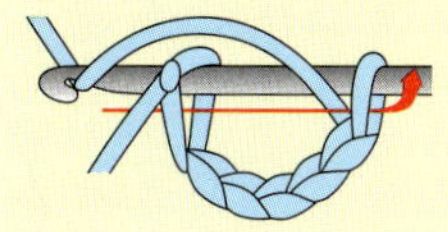

Chain color change (ch color change) Yo with new color, draw through last lp on hook.

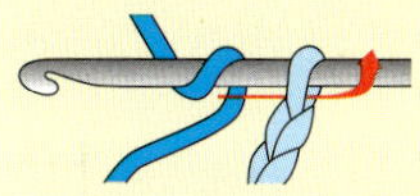

Double crochet color change (dc color change) Drop first color, yo with new color, draw through last 2 lps of st.

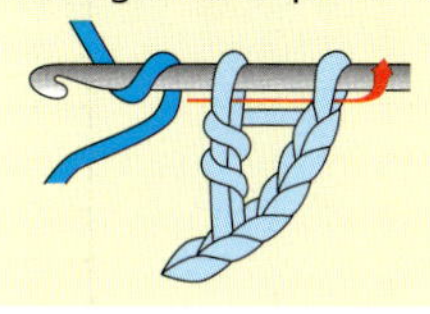

Treble crochet (tr): Yo twice, insert hook in st, yo, pull through st, [yo, pull through 2 lps] 3 times.

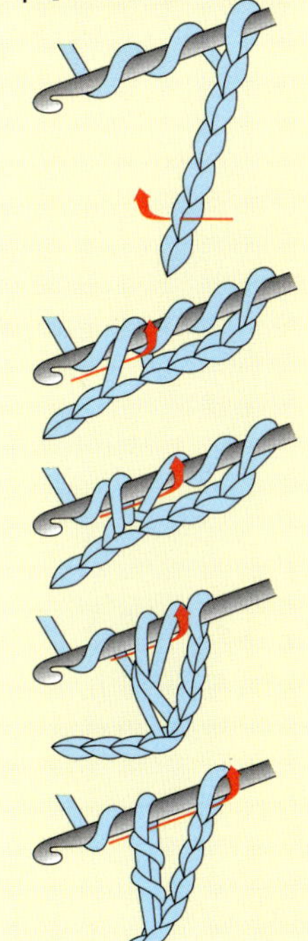

Single crochet decrease (sc dec): (Insert hook, yo, draw lp through) in each of the sts indicated, yo, draw through all lps on hook.

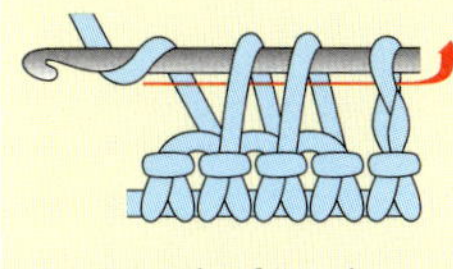

Example of 2-sc dec

Half double crochet decrease (hdc dec): (Yo, insert hook, yo, draw lp through) in each of the sts indicated, yo, draw through all lps on hook.

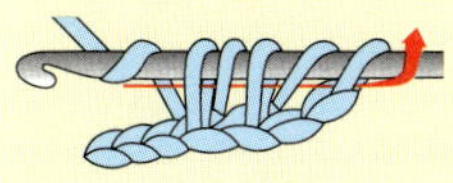

Example of 2-hdc dec

Double crochet decrease (dc dec): (Yo, insert hook, yo, draw lp through, yo, draw through 2 lps on hook) in each of the sts indicated, yo, draw through all lps on hook.

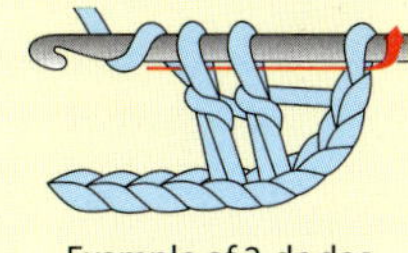

Example of 2-dc dec

Treble crochet decrease (tr dec): Holding back last lp of each st, tr in each of the sts indicated, yo, pull through all lps on hook.

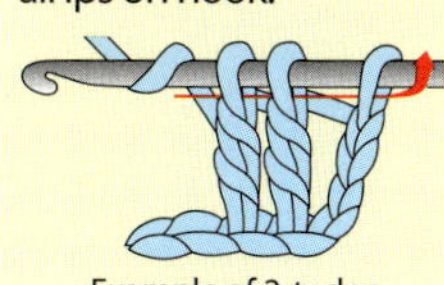

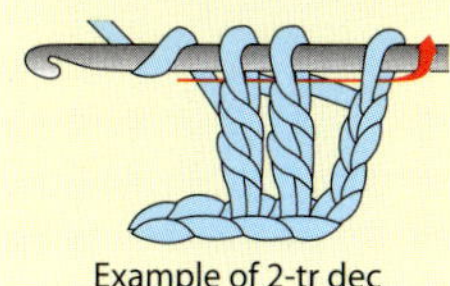

Example of 2-tr dec

Metric Conversion Charts

METRIC CONVERSIONS				
yards	x	.9144	=	metres (m)
yards	x	91.44	=	centimetres (cm)
inches	x	2.54	=	centimetres (cm)
inches	x	25.40	=	millimetres (mm)
inches	x	.0254	=	metres (m)

centimetres	x	.3937	=	inches
metres	x	1.0936	=	yards

INCHES INTO MILLIMETRES & CENTIMETRES (Rounded off slightly)

inches	mm	cm	inches	cm	inches	cm	inches	cm
1/8	3	0.3	5	12.5	21	53.5	38	96.5
1/4	6	0.6	5 1/2	14	22	56	39	99
3/8	10	1	6	15	23	58.5	40	101.5
1/2	13	1.3	7	18	24	61	41	104
5/8	15	1.5	8	20.5	25	63.5	42	106.5
3/4	20	2	9	23	26	66	43	109
7/8	22	2.2	10	25.5	27	68.5	44	112
1	25	2.5	11	28	28	71	45	114.5
1 1/4	32	3.2	12	30.5	29	73.5	46	117
1 1/2	38	3.8	13	33	30	76	47	119.5
1 3/4	45	4.5	14	35.5	31	79	48	122
2	50	5	15	38	32	81.5	49	124.5
2 1/2	65	6.5	16	40.5	33	84	50	127
3	75	7.5	17	43	34	86.5		
3 1/2	90	9	18	46	35	89		
4	100	10	19	48.5	36	91.5		
4 1/2	115	11.5	20	51	37	94		

KNITTING NEEDLES CONVERSION CHART

Canada/U.S.	0	1	2	3	4	5	6	7	8	9	10	10½	11	13	15
Metric (mm)	2	2¼	2¾	3¼	3½	3¾	4	4½	5	5½	6	6½	8	9	10

CROCHET HOOKS CONVERSION CHART

Canada/U.S.	1/B	2/C	3/D	4/E	5/F	6/G	8/H	9/I	10/J	10½/K	N
Metric (mm)	2.25	2.75	3.25	3.5	3.75	4.25	5	5.5	6	6.5	9.0

Annie's®

Precious Cocoons is published by Annie's, 306 East Parr Road, Berne, IN 46711. Printed in USA. Copyright © 2015 Annie's. All rights reserved. This publication may not be reproduced in part or in whole without written permission from the publisher.

RETAIL STORES: If you would like to carry this publication or any other Annie's publication, visit AnniesWSL.com.

Every effort has been made to ensure that the instructions in this publication are complete and accurate. We cannot, however, take responsibility for human error, typographical mistakes or variations in individual work. Please visit AnniesCustomerService.com to check for pattern updates.

ISBN: 978-1-57367-925-1

1 2 3 4 5 6 7 8 9